BOOK 2

MOVIE & TV HITS
for TEENS

9 GRADED SELECTIONS
FOR INTERMEDIATE PIANISTS

ARRANGED BY DAN COATES

The *Movie & TV Hits for Teens* series presents carefully leveled, accessible arrangements for the teenage pianist. This series provides students with the opportunity to develop their technique and musicianship while performing popular pieces from their favorite movies and television shows.

CONTENTS

Alfred

Produced by
Alfred Music
P.O. Box 10003
Van Nuys, CA 91410-0003
alfred.com

Printed in USA.

ISBN-10: 1-4706-3805-3
ISBN-13: 978-1-4706-3805-4

THE BIG BANG THEORY
(Main Title)

Words and Music by Ed Robertson
Arr. Dan Coates

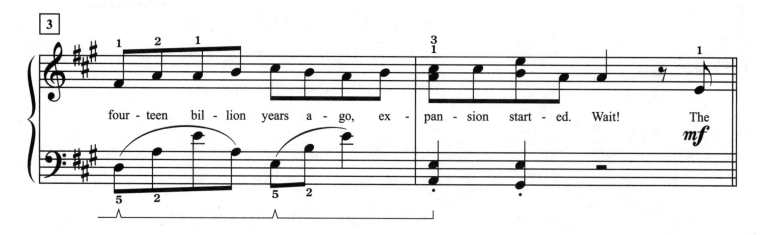

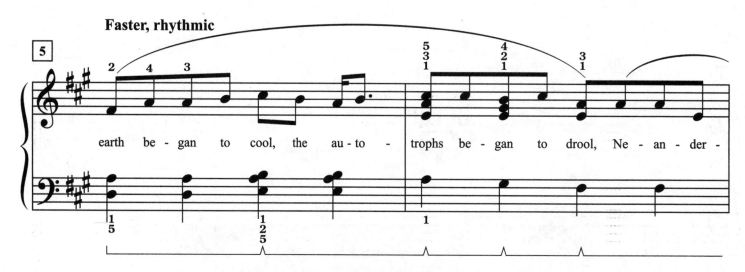

3

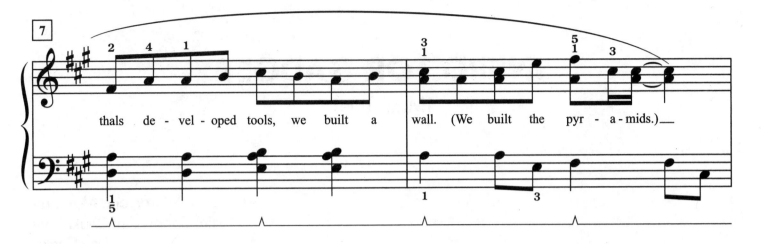

4

INSPECTOR GADGET
(Main Title)

Words and Music by
Haim Saban and Shuki Levy
Arr. Dan Coates

Moderately fast

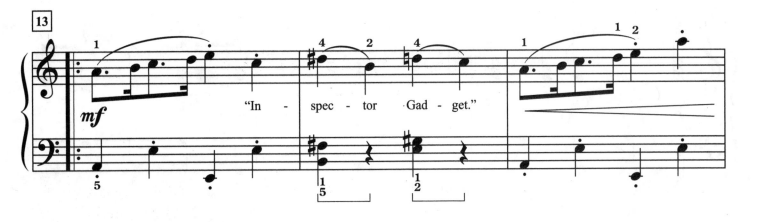

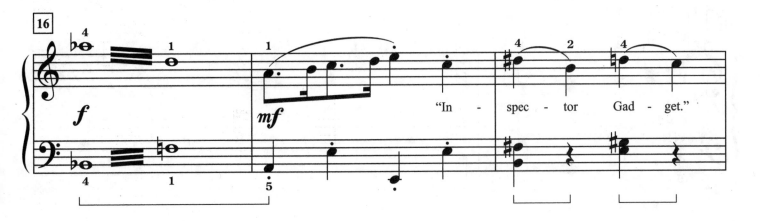

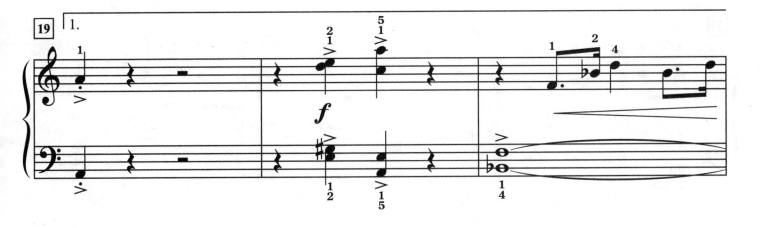

"Go,   Gad - get,   go."

_f_

simile

"Go,   Gad - get,   go."

_mf_

"In -

spec - tor Gad - get."

_f_

IN DREAMS

(from *The Lord of the Rings: The Fellowship of the Ring*)

Words and Music by
Fran Walsh and Howard Shore
Arr. Dan Coates

TIME

(from *Inception*)

Composed by Hans Zimmer
Arr. Dan Coates

14

JUST LIKE FIRE

(from *Alice Through the Looking Glass*)

Words and Music by Oscar Holter,
Max Martin, Shellback and Alecia Moore
Arr. Dan Coates

© 2016 WOLF COUSINS, WARNER/CHAPPELL MUSIC SCANDINAVIA AB, MXM MUSIC AB, PINK INSIDE PUBLISHING, EMI BLACKWOOD MUSIC, INC.,
WALT DISNEY MUSIC COMPANY, WONDERLAND MUSIC COMPANY, INC. and LIONHEART MUSIC AB
All Rights on behalf of WOLF COUSINS and WARNER/CHAPPELL MUSIC SCANDINAVIA AB Administered by WB MUSIC CORP.
All Rights on behalf of MXM MUSIC AB Administered by KOBALT SONGS MUSIC PUBLISHING
All Rights on behalf of itself and PINK INSIDE PUBLISHING Administered by EMI BLACKWOOD MUSIC, INC.
All Rights Reserved

17

A MAN AND HIS BEASTS

(from *Fantastic Beasts and Where to Find Them*)

Composed by James Newton Howard
Arr. Dan Coates

THE PINK PANTHER

(from *The Pink Panther*)

By Henry Mancini
Arr. Dan Coates

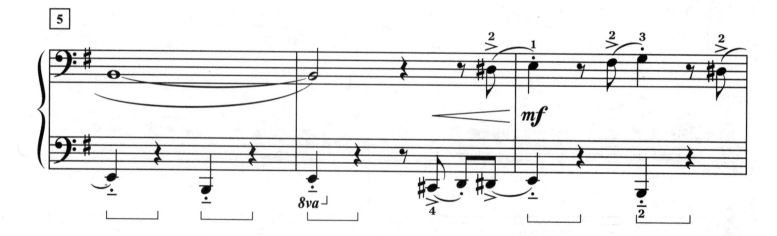

* Imitate the sound of double bass pizzicatos.

UNDER THE SEA

(from Walt Disney's *The Little Mermaid*)

Lyrics by Howard Ashman
Music by Alan Menken
Arr. Dan Coates

Brightly, with a calypso beat

28

SLEDGEHAMMER

(from *Star Trek Beyond*)

Words and Music by Robyn Fenty,
Sia Furler and Jesse Shatkin
Arr. Dan Coates

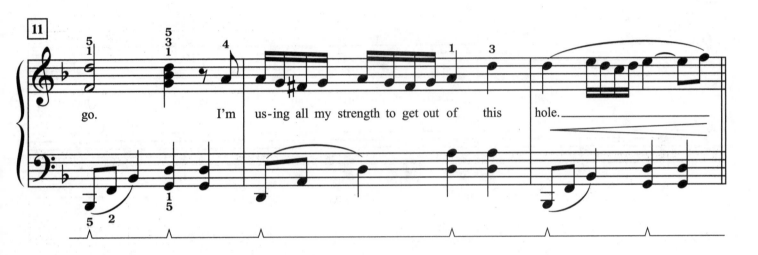

And on the floor __ I'd be ly-ing cold, life-less. But I hit a wall, __ I hit a

wall, watched it fall. _____ You're just an-oth-er brick and I'm a sledge-ham-mer, __

to Coda ⊕

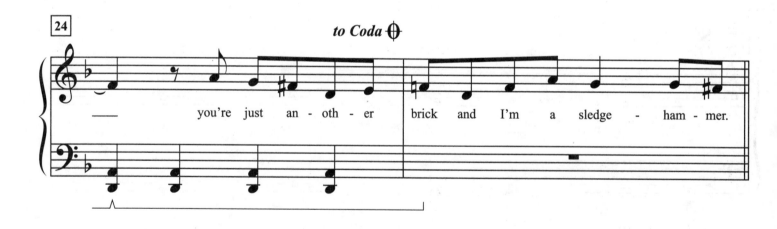

—— you're just an-oth-er brick and I'm a sledge - ham - mer.

mp I hit a wall, I prayed that I would make it through, __ make it through. ____

I can't sur - vive a life that's with - out you,___ that's with - out you,___ yeah.

And I will rise___ up from__ ash - es now,___ the ash - es now.___

Oh, the spar - row flies with just the crumbs of lov - ing spilled.__ I was

brac - ing for the pain___ and then I let it go. I

D.S. al Coda

gath-ered all my strength and I found my - self whole.

Coda

brick and I'm a sledge - ham - mer. You're just an - oth - er

brick and I'm a sledge - ham-mer, you're just an - oth - er brick and I'm a sledge - ham-mer.

mp *dim.* *pp*